INSPIRING STORIES FOR CHILDREN

Volume 1

Bal-Mukund Character Building Series

Bal-Mukund Coordinator: Aruna Kannan
Editorial Team: Shreya Bhat, Anand Rao
Contributing Authors: Amita Sinha, Saurabh Turakhia
Illustration & Design: Graphics Spot

Published by:
Jagadguru Kripalu Yog
7405 Stoney Point Drive
Plano, TX 75025
USA
www.jkyog.org

ISBN 978-0-9826675-0-7

Printed by:

Elegant Prints

www.elegant-prints.com

Dedication

The Bal-Mukund Character Building Series is dedicated to our Beloved Spiritual Master, Jagadguru Shree Kripaluji Maharaj, who is illuminating this world with the purest rays of Divine knowledge and love.

He has taught us by his example, the importance of nurturing children with love and care, to help them realize a glorious future. He has given us the supreme process of building a noble value system into impressionable young minds by teaching them selfless Divine love.

We pray that by his blessings this series will be helpful in inspiring, elevating and molding the children of today, who in turn will create a better world for tomorrow.

Jagadguru Shree Kripaluji Maharaj

MESSAGE FROM SHREE MAHARAJJI

पवित्र जीवन एवं महान व्यक्तित्व की नींव की प्राप्ति के हेतु बाल्यावस्था में ही दिये गये संस्कारों से पड़ती है। अतएव माता पिता द्वारा बच्चों को सर्वश्रेष्ठ प्रेमोपहार यही होता है कि उन्हें बचपन से ही दैवी गुण संपन्न बनाया जाय।

उन दैवी गुणों का प्राकट्य, परमात्मा की निष्काम भक्ति द्वारा अंतःकरण की शुद्धि से ही होता है।

अतः आध्यात्मिक शिक्षा द्वारा बच्चों के मन में भगवद् भक्ति का संचार करना उनके उज्वल भविष्य के हेतु सर्वाधिक कल्याणकारी है।

भक्त प्रह्लाद ने कहा था -

कौमार आचरेत्प्राज्ञो धर्मान् भागवतानिह (भागवत ७/६/१)

अर्थात् बाल्यावस्था से ही भागवत धर्म का अनुसरण प्रारंभ कर देना चाहिये।

यह बाल मुकुंद चरित्र निर्माण पुस्तक माला भारतीय संस्कृति एवं शास्त्रों वेदों पर आधारित ऐसी ही कल्याणकारी आध्यात्मिक-शिक्षायुक्त है। मेरी शुभकामना है कि बालवृंद इस से अवश्य लाभान्वित होंगे।

भवदीय - जगद्गुरु कृपालु महाराज

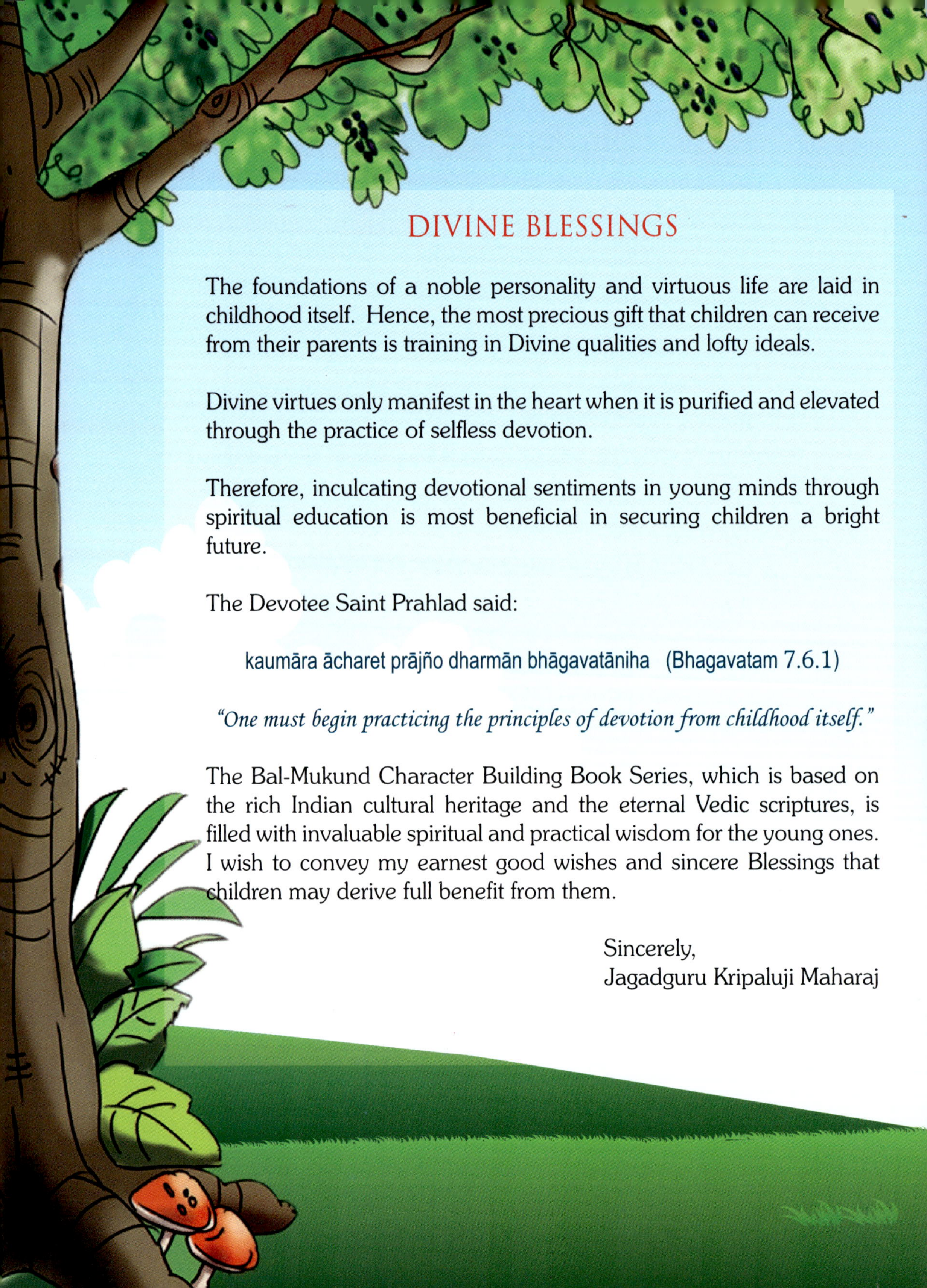

DIVINE BLESSINGS

The foundations of a noble personality and virtuous life are laid in childhood itself. Hence, the most precious gift that children can receive from their parents is training in Divine qualities and lofty ideals.

Divine virtues only manifest in the heart when it is purified and elevated through the practice of selfless devotion.

Therefore, inculcating devotional sentiments in young minds through spiritual education is most beneficial in securing children a bright future.

The Devotee Saint Prahlad said:

kaumāra ācharet prājño dharmān bhāgavatāniha (Bhagavatam 7.6.1)

"One must begin practicing the principles of devotion from childhood itself."

The Bal-Mukund Character Building Book Series, which is based on the rich Indian cultural heritage and the eternal Vedic scriptures, is filled with invaluable spiritual and practical wisdom for the young ones. I wish to convey my earnest good wishes and sincere Blessings that children may derive full benefit from them.

Sincerely,
Jagadguru Kripaluji Maharaj

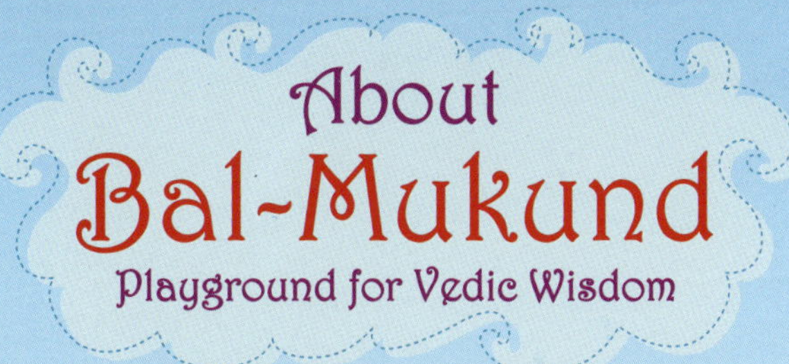

Bal-Mukund is a specially designed personality development program for children, envisioned by Swami Mukundananda. It endeavors to:

- ❖ Educate young minds in the knowledge of Vedic wisdom to lead a virtuous life.
- ❖ Enthuse the spirit of giving with a service attitude.
- ❖ Encourage problem solving with courage, confidence and faith.
- ❖ Entertain creativity, expand power of concentration and focus.
- ❖ Elevate young minds to higher consciousness and fill their hearts with love and reverence for God.

The Bal-Mukund program is designed for the holistic development of a young one's physical, intellectual, social and spiritual faculties. Activities include Yoga, Pranayam, Meditation for children, Shlokas, Kirtans, Stories/discussion, Games, Language classes, Arts and Crafts.

For Bal-Mukund program details and centers:
www.bal-mukund.org

INTRODUCTION TO THE BAL-MUKUND CHARACTER BUILDING SERIES

The mark of a civilized society is the loving care it takes of its children. They are not merely children; they will soon be other people's husbands and wives, and parents of grandchildren. They possess God's life force that is yearning to make them Presidents, Scientists, Engineers, Doctors, Artists, Writers, and Musicians. Just as the acorn carries the potential of becoming an oak tree, children carry in them infinite potential for future greatness. Caring parents and teachers see this potential, and carefully cultivate and nurture it.

Parents and teachers are partners of God. They are working with the Creator of the Universe in shaping human nature and forging the future world. Each day they make deposits in the memory banks of their children. These deposits must be uplifting, and ennobling to their impressionable minds, which are sponge-like and very sensitive to the impressions they receive from their mentors. Children possess a remarkable amount of passion to go after their ideals. They throw themselves completely, heart and soul, into everything. The impressions they receive in these formative years mould their vision for the future. Loving parents and teachers teach their children to dream with their eyes open, of a noble and fulfilling life. They fill their hearts with lofty ideals and inspiring thoughts, and then fondly watch as their wards strive to attain the goals that have been mapped in them in their childhood.

Jagadguru Shree Kripaluji Maharaj teaches that best inheritance we can leave for children is good training in character building. A strong and sound value system built into them will remain until death. It will be the foundation for a successful and rewarding life. Hence, the values we inspire them to cherish are of paramount importance.

Children must be taught that money and luxurious possessions alone will not give happiness, but a virtuous life will be a continual feast.

Time spent in inculcating such values in children is an investment into the future. It is the finest gift of love from parents to their children. The Bal-Mukund Character Building Series contains invaluable instructions, famous verses, bhajans, stories, life histories and information about festivals, for building values in children. For ease of remembrance, the values that are required for triumph in life have been grouped with the letters of the acronym "KRIPALU". These set of values will teach children to be heroic from within, and instill nobleness in their thought, word and deed.

The compendium of stories, biographies, festivals, sayings, kirtans and prayers in this series of books has been chosen from the Vedic scriptures and the rich literary heritage of India. They convey powerful messages to educate, encourage, enthuse, and entertain young minds. Most importantly, they fill the heart with love and reverence for God, which is the essence of all morality. We hope they will be cherished by teachers, parents and children alike, who will meditate upon them, learn them and make them a part of their lives.

Swami Mukundananda

The "KRIPALU" Values

K for Kindness

Helping nature, Service attitude, Caring for others, Compassionate to the sufferings of others, Non-violence towards all beings, Forgiveness, and Seeing the Divinity in others.

R for Respect

Respect for Elders, Respect for Teachers, Respect for Authority, Respect for each other, Courtesy, Good Manners, Not seeing faults in others, Being non-judgmental, Acceptance of the differing viewpoints of others, Obedience to Elders and Authority

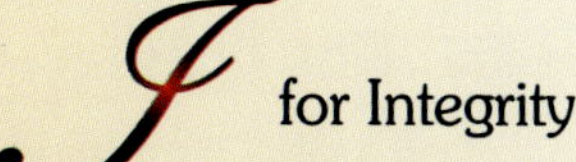

I for Integrity

Truthfulness, Purity of thoughts and intentions, Self-discipline and control over mind and senses, Restraint from temptation, Restraint from harmful influences like drugs, cigarettes, and alcohol, restraint from gambling, Associating with good people and giving up association of those who are a bad influence.

for Perseverance

Hardworking, Enduring, Patient, Dedication to the work at hand, Tenacity to bear difficulties and not give up, Overcoming obstacles through persistence, Keeping a positive "I can do it" attitude, Single-mindedness towards goal, Using tact and intelligence and mental power to solve a problem.

for Accountability

Taking full responsibility for ones deeds, Taking the onus for mistakes, Responsibility for correcting them, not blaming others or having a whining nature, Taking responsibility for organizing oneself and one's work, Accepting the law of karma that what happens to us is a result of our own actions, Being punctual to our time commitments.

for Love for God

Trust in God, Faith in His protection, Acceptance of His will, Keeping a positive attitude in every situation with Faith in His Grace, A Sense of Gratitude for all that God has given us, Belief that He is with us and watching us always, Doing all actions for His pleasure, unconditional devotion to Him.

for Unassuming

Modesty, Unpretentiousness, Simplicity, Humility, Not boasting or showing off, Reverence for the Greatness of God, Faith that everything belongs to God and not to us, Realizing that God has a grand scheme why things happen and we all have a tiny role to play in His design.

Story Index

K for Kindness

The Kripalu value beginning with the letter "K" is Kindness. The various aspects of kindness are:

❖ Helping nature

❖ Service attitude

❖ Caring for others

❖ Compassionate to the sufferings of others

❖ Non-violence towards all beings

❖ Forgiveness

❖ Seeing the Divinity in others.

The Fox and the Stork

A fox and a stork were neighbors as well as friends. The fox used to laugh secretly at the stork's looks. He wanted to amuse himself by playing a trick on the stork.

One day, he said to the stork, “I am going to make some soup today. Come and have dinner at my place.” The stork replied, “Thanks very much. I love soup. I will meet you for dinner.”

The stork arrived at the right time. She was very hungry and could smell the soup. She said, “The soup smells so good.” The fox served dinner. He placed two flat dishes full of soup. While he lapped up the soup with enjoyment, the stork could have nothing. She could only wet the end of her long bill and stayed hungry. The fox said, “I think you did not like the soup. I am sorry.” The stork understood the fox’s trick but did not get angry. She said, “Do not be sorry for me. Come and have dinner with me one day.” The fox accepted with pleasure.

After a few days, the fox went to the stork’s house for dinner. He

could smell the food being cooked in the kitchen, which made him very hungry. He waited for his dinner. The stork served dinner in two long jars with a narrow mouth and ate easily from the jar, while the fox remained hungry. He could only enjoy the smell and licked the mouth of the jar from outside.

The hungry fox got angry and said, "How can I eat from this jar?" The stork replied, "Well, you served soup on a flat dish. I came back hungry from your house. You should not have played that trick on me, unless you are ready for the same treatment yourself. If you cheat anyone, you will be cheated too. You had no kindness for me. Your wrongdoing has bounced back on you. Now you know how I felt."

Moral of the story

Moral 1: Understand others' needs. Do not be mean to others.

Moral 2: Do unto others, as you would have them do unto you.

The Wind and the Sun

Once, the wind and the sun had an argument. "I am far stronger than you," boasted the wind. The sun replied, "There is great strength in gentleness. I may be gentle, but I am more powerful than you." They decided upon a wager. The sun said, "Let us have a contest and see who is stronger."

Far below, a traveler was going on a winding road. He was wearing a warm cloak. The sun said, "Let us see who can remove the cloak from the man."

The wind bragged, "It will be quite simple for me to force him to remove his cloak." The sun did not say anything. The wind wanted to try first. He blew hard down the road. The birds clung to trees. Everywhere dust and leaves were flying here and there.

The man shivered in the wind and clutched his cloak tightly to himself. The wind blew even harder, and the man wrapped his cloak more tightly around him and clung to it.

In the end, the wind got tired and gave up. He said to the sun, "If I could not remove the man's cloak, you will never be able to. There is no need to try. Let us end the contest."

The sun said, "Well, I want to try too. There is no use in giving up without trying." The wind did not argue because he was sure the sun would not succeed where he had failed.

The sun was hiding behind a cloud. Now he came out and began to beam. At first, he shone very gently and this made the traveler loosen the cloak. After that, he shone brighter and it started becoming warm. Finally, the sun began shining even brighter, and the traveler felt hot. He took off his cloak, put it in his bag and sat under the shade of a tree.

The wind accepted defeat. He said to the sun, "How did you make the man take off his cloak?"

The sun replied, "It was easy. Through gentleness, I got my way." Gentle persuasion is often more effective than brute force.

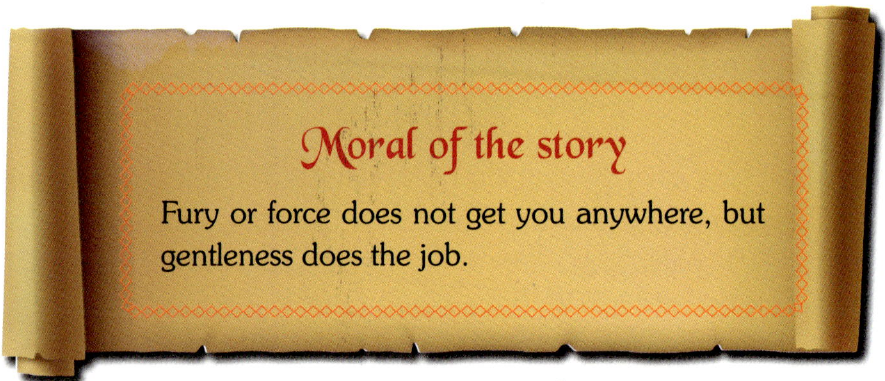

Moral of the story

Fury or force does not get you anywhere, but gentleness does the job.

The Miser

Once upon a time, there lived a miser called Motilal. He had a lot of money, but did not like spending it. He did not help anyone with money, even though he had many gold coins.

Motilal refused to share his wealth with anyone, including his family, friends, servants or other poor people. His family was not happy with the way he led his life. He cared little for his wife and kid, and did not fulfill his responsibilities as a good householder. He did not listen to his wife and asked her to stay away from money matters.

One day, their son fell ill. Motilal's wife asked him to call a doctor immediately to examine her son. He flatly refused to get a doctor and said that doctors are not good anymore. His wife was very unhappy and went to the doctor on her own.

After some time, Motilal melted all the coins and made a big block of gold. He was very happy to see the gold block, but he was scared that someone might try to steal the gold from him. Therefore, he dug a pit in the ground of his house and buried the gold block deep down into the pit. He covered the mouth of the pit nicely so that no one would be able to find it. Every day, he would come to the pit and dig it up to see his block of gold. After being satisfied to see it there, he would cover it up again.

One night, someone came and stole the gold block. Motilal found out that his gold was missing and started crying. A friend saw him

sitting near the pit and crying. He said, "What is the use of burying gold in a pit and looking at it every day? It was like a stone to you. When you had money, you did not spend it but hid it in a pit. Now it is stolen and you have nothing left. If you had shared your wealth with others, you would not be sad today."

The miser could have been kind to others. He could have helped them by sharing his money. Others would have benefitted from it, and he too would be happy. Now he had lost everything.

Motilal realized his folly and cursed himself for being a miser. He repented for being insensitive and not helping others. He had valued wealth more than his family and society. He decided to mend his ways and stop being a miser. He realized the value of having a caring family and sharing wealth with others.

Moral of the story

The greatest joy comes from sharing what you have, and not from keeping everything for one's own selfish needs

R for Respect

The Kripalu Value beginning with the letter "R" is Respect. The various aspects of respect are:

- ❖ Respect for Elders
- ❖ Respect for Teachers
- ❖ Respect for Authority
- ❖ Respect for each other
- ❖ Courtesy
- ❖ Good Manners

Shravan Kumar - The Noble Son

Once upon a time, there lived a boy named Shravan Kumar. His parents were poor, old and blind, but they raised him well. Shravan Kumar was strong, healthy, honest and well-mannered. He respected his parents. He did everything for his mother and father with a lot of sincerity and love, fulfilled all their wishes, and kept them happy.

One day, Shravan's parents expressed their desire to go on a pilgrimage. The dutiful Shravan decided to fulfill their wish. He wanted his parents to have a comfortable trip. So he made a big weighing balance. He tied two big baskets to the end of a pole with ropes and made his parents sit on it. He carried this pole on his shoulders and started on the journey with his mother and father sitting in the basket. The parents were very proud of their son's efforts.

On their way to the pilgrimage, they reached the forest of Ayodhya and rested for a while. Shravan's parents were thirsty. They requested him to get water to quench their thirst. Shravan immediately set his parents under the shade of the tree and took a vessel to fetch water from the river Saryu.

In the meantime, Dashrath, the king of Ayodhya was hunting in the same forest. He had come all alone. He had a very special talent. He could shoot any animal that made the slightest sound with his bow and arrow, without even seeing the animal. Dashrath heard Shravan filling water in his vessel. He thought it was a deer drinking water and shot the arrow in the direction of the sound. The arrow pierced Shravan's heart. He gave out a cry and fell to the ground.

On hearing the scream, king Dashrath ran to the river bank to see who it was. He saw Shravan Kumar crying in pain. King Dashrath became very sad. He was angry with himself for making such a big mistake.

When Shravan saw the king, he called out to him and said, "I came to take water for my parents. They are very thirsty. I will be ever grateful to you if you can carry some water to my parents and tell them the sad news." He died soon after.

When king Dashrath gave Shravan Kumar's parents the water to drink, they refused to accept it. Though blind, they knew he was not their son. The king sadly told them what had happened to their son. Shravan's old and blind parents were shocked. They became very sad. They cursed the king that he too would meet his death in the sorrow of separation from his son, just as he had done to them. They cried out loud and told the king to take them to their son.

King Dashrath carried them on his shoulders to the place where he had shot Shravan. As they sat crying near his body, they heard Shravan speak, "Through my services to you, I have attained a place in heaven. Do not worry about me. I will wait for you both and serve you when you come here."

Even today, we remember Shravan Kumar as the ideal son who honored, loved and took care of his parents till the end.

Moral of the story

Respect and love your parents and elders. Help them in whatever way you can.

Remember that your parents love you and always have your best interests at heart.

The Lion and the Mouse

One day a lion was sleeping in the jungle. A mouse that was passing by accidently stepped over the sleeping lion.

The lion grabbed the mouse and roared in anger, holding him in his large claws. "Do you know who I am? I am the king of the jungle. How dare you disturb my slumber! I will kill you."

"Spare me sir. Please do not kill me. If you let me go, one day I may be able to help you too," said the mouse trembling with fear. "You are so small. How can you be of any use to me?" said the lion scornfully. "But I will let you go since you were brave enough to appeal." "Oh thank you, Your Majesty!" squeaked the mouse, and scurried away as fast as he could.

A few days later, the lion was caught in a hunter's net. No matter how hard the lion tried, he could not break free. Instead, he became even more tangled in the net of ropes.

He began roaring for help. The mouse heard the lion's cry for help and quickly went to his rescue. He managed to cut a big hole in the net by nibbling with his teeth and set the lion free.

"I did not believe that you could be of use to me, but today you saved my life," said the lion humbly and thanked the mouse for his help.

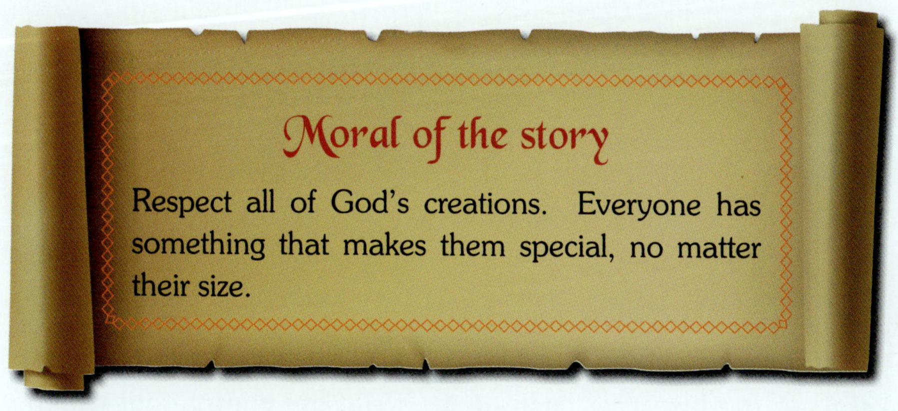

Moral of the story

Respect all of God's creations. Everyone has something that makes them special, no matter their size.

The Mischievous Boy

Balu was a young, clever and mischievous boy. He wasted his talent on wrong acts. His favorite pass time was to fool people. Balu never missed a chance to anger people by making them look foolish.

One day, he saw the barber shaving a person's beard in a saloon. An idea struck him to irritate the barber. He went to the barber and asked, "How much do you charge for a shave?"

The barber was very surprised to see a young boy asking for a shave. Balu had no beard on his face at all. The barber replied, "Five rupees." Hearing this, Balu gave him a five rupee note and sat in the saloon chair.

The barber did not know what to do, but he knew the boy was up to something. The barber decided to teach Balu a lesson. He wrapped a towel around Balu's neck and prepared the shaving lather gently applying it on Balu's face. He left him to attend to another customer.

Balu waited for a long time but the barber ignored him completely. He kept serving his other customers. Balu grew impatient sitting with his face in foam.

"Hey barber! I have been waiting here for a long time for you to shave me." The barber looked at him and replied, "Sir, I am waiting for your beard to grow before shaving it."

Balu did not know what to say. His own naughty thought had turned against him. He also learned a good lesson not to fool people again.

Moral of the story

Learn to respect others and treat them the way you want to be treated.

Obey your Parents

Once upon a time, a fawn lived with his mother. He was not allowed to go anywhere alone. The fawn thought that he was grown up and he did not need his mother to accompany him everywhere. He felt that he could have fun if he went alone, and decided to go without telling his mother.

One hot sunny day, while the fawn's mother was sleeping, he slipped out by himself. He went to an open field where he played happily. After some time, he became thirsty and went to drink water at a nearby stream.

When he had finished drinking, he saw a lion standing upstream. The lion was staring at the fawn with red burning eyes. The lion licked his lips, and the poor fawn knew the lion was planning to eat him. He began trembling with fear. He did not know how to save himself from the lion.

The lion said, "Why did you drink water from this stream? You have made it dirty. How will I drink water now?" The frightened fawn started moving back slowly. "Sir, I am not the one who has made this water dirty. The stream is flowing from upwards, where you are standing. From there, it is coming down towards me," replied the fawn.

The lion kept quiet after the fawn's reply. He started thinking of

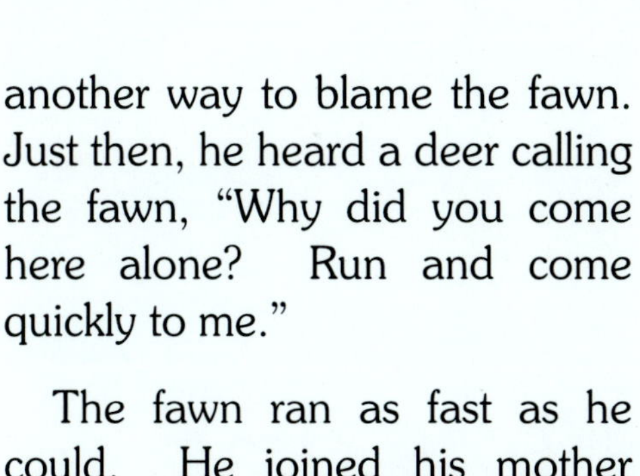

another way to blame the fawn. Just then, he heard a deer calling the fawn, "Why did you come here alone? Run and come quickly to me."

The fawn ran as fast as he could. He joined his mother who was waiting. Together they disappeared into the forest and the lion was left disappointed. The fawn was very thankful that his mother had found him on time. He made up his mind never to go out alone. From that day on, the fawn decided that he would always respect and obey his mother. Only then he would not get into any trouble.

Moral of the story

Respect, love and obey your parents. Remember that your parents love you very much. The rules they require you to follow are for your own good because they care.

Good Manners and Good Habits

Good manners and good habits are important for a healthy mind and body. Good health is very important for doing well in school, and later, when you grow up. Moreover, everyone likes people who have good manners and good habits. That is why children must work hard to develop good habits at a very young age.

Can you imagine what would happen to your teeth, if you did not

brush them daily? Germs and bacteria would decay your teeth and they would fall off quickly. Brushing teeth is an example of a good habit. Some other examples of good habits you need to develop for yourself are:

- Wash hands before eating anything.
- Take a bath daily for cleansing the body, and wearing clean clothes.
- Eat many green vegetables and do not waste food.
- Do yoga, pranayam and other exercises to keep yourself physically fit.
- Practice devotion to God. Make time to pray to Him at least twice a day and thank Him for everything you have.

- Sleep well – early to bed and early to rise.

Through good habits, you show respect to yourself and to people around you. Examples of good habits you should develop to show respect to others are:

- Be polite to others, especially your elders.
- Use the magic words "Please" and "Thank you."
- Share what you have with others, especially with those who are needy.

- Always speak the truth.
- Say "Sorry," if you are wrong.
- Do not hurt others, even animals or insects.
- Do not fight with friends and family members. Learn to love others
- Try to help others, at home, in school, in your immediate surroundings and the community.

These are some of the important habits you need to develop. These habits will make you a healthier and better human being. You will then be liked and respected by all.

Namaste

Namaste is the Indian way of greeting each other. Whenever and wherever Indians meet, at home, on the street or on a bus, they always greet each other with a Namaste. Even before they start a conversation, they begin by saying "Namaste." This is the greeting for all Indians - men and women, young and old, friends and strangers.

The Meaning of Namaste

In Sanskrit, Namaste means, "I bow to you." While saying it, the head is bowed down and the hands are folded together. By bowing down the head, the person saying Namaste expresses love, respect and friendship.

Namaste in Prayers

During prayers, Indians bow their heads and close their eyes, while doing Namaste to God. It means that they are offering their respects to God who is seated in their hearts. While doing Namaste to God, they usually say God's name too, such as "Ram Ram" or "Jai Shree Krishna."

Namaste to People

According to Hinduism, God is in every person. By saying Namaste,

we recognize the presence of God in the other person. By folding our hands, we offer our respects to God seated within that person.

Other Meanings of Namaste

There are other meanings of Namaste too. Namaste requires that we place the five fingers of the left hand exactly next to the five fingers of the right hand. The five fingers of the left hand represent the five senses of karma, or our actions, while the five fingers of the right hand represent the five organs of knowledge. Hence, Namaste means that our actions must be governed by rightful knowledge. In other words, this is a reminder for us to think and act in the right manner.

During the Namaste greeting, when the five fingers of both the hands are held together, a total of ten is achieved. The number ten is a sign of perfection and unity. Namaste is a way of conveying good wishes to the other person to attain perfection and harmony.

So next time you see an Indian, bow your head slightly, fold your hands and say Namaste.

I for Integrity

The Kripalu value beginning with the letter "I" is Integrity. The various aspects of integrity are:

- ❖ Truthfulness
- ❖ Purity of thoughts and intentions
- ❖ Self-discipline and control over mind and senses
- ❖ Restraint from temptation
- ❖ Restraint from harmful influences like drugs cigarettes, and alcohol
- ❖ Restraint from gambling
- ❖ Associating with good people
- ❖ Giving up association of those who are a bad influence.

The Angel and the Woodcutter

Once there lived a poor woodcutter with his wife and children in a small hut. He made his living by cutting and selling wood from the forest with his iron axe. He sold wood in the nearby village and bought food for his family. Though he was poor, the woodcutter led a contented life. He was happy with whatever he could earn with his hard efforts.

One day, the woodcutter woke up early. He prayed and thanked Almighty God for keeping him safe and healthy. He then bid farewell to his wife and children and set off to work with his handy axe resting on his shoulders.

On that day, the woodcutter had chosen to cut an old tree. The tree grew beside the river. As he raised his hands to chop the tree's branches, the axe slipped away from his fingers and fell into the flowing river.

The woodcutter was sad and had no idea how to get his axe back. The river was too deep and he did not know how to swim. He thought about his wife and children at home. If he failed to sell wood, they would all go hungry.

As he sat under the tree, an angel appeared before him and asked why he was so unhappy. The woodcutter told her about his problem. "Oh angel, I will forever be grateful to you if you bring back my axe that has fallen into the river."

Pleased by his manners, the angel dived into the river. She came out with a sparkling golden axe. "Is this the axe you lost?" she asked. "No" replied the woodcutter disappointed. "My axe is not made of gold."

The angel dived again and came up with a shining silver axe. "Is this the one?" she asked the woodcutter. "No" he replied. "My axe is not made of silver either; it hardly shines."

For the third time, the angel dived into the river. This time, she came out with the woodcutter's iron axe, much to his delight. The woodcutter said, "That is my axe! I am very thankful for your help; how can I repay you? I do not have anything."

The angel said, "I am pleased with your honesty. You could have claimed the gold and silver axe as your own and taken it home. However, you did not lie to me. Instead, you chose the iron axe that rightfully belonged to you. For your honesty, I reward you with both the golden and silver axes." Saying this, she handed him all the three axes and disappeared before he could thank her for his good fortune.

The woodcutter returned home a very happy man. He was rewarded for his honesty and hard work. His family was happy to learn what had happened that day.

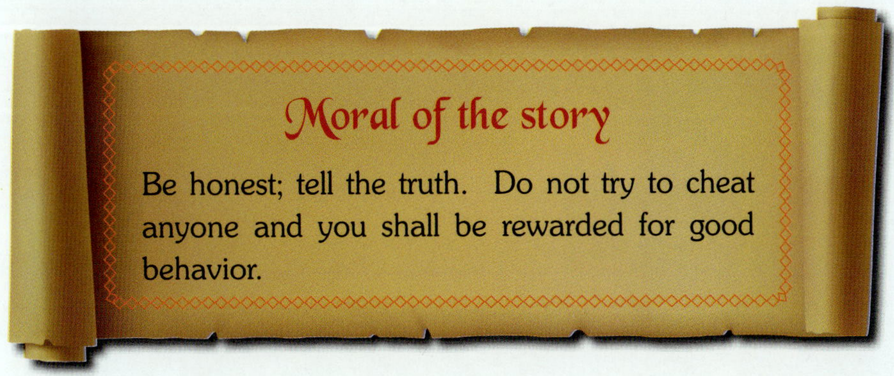

Moral of the story

Be honest; tell the truth. Do not try to cheat anyone and you shall be rewarded for good behavior.

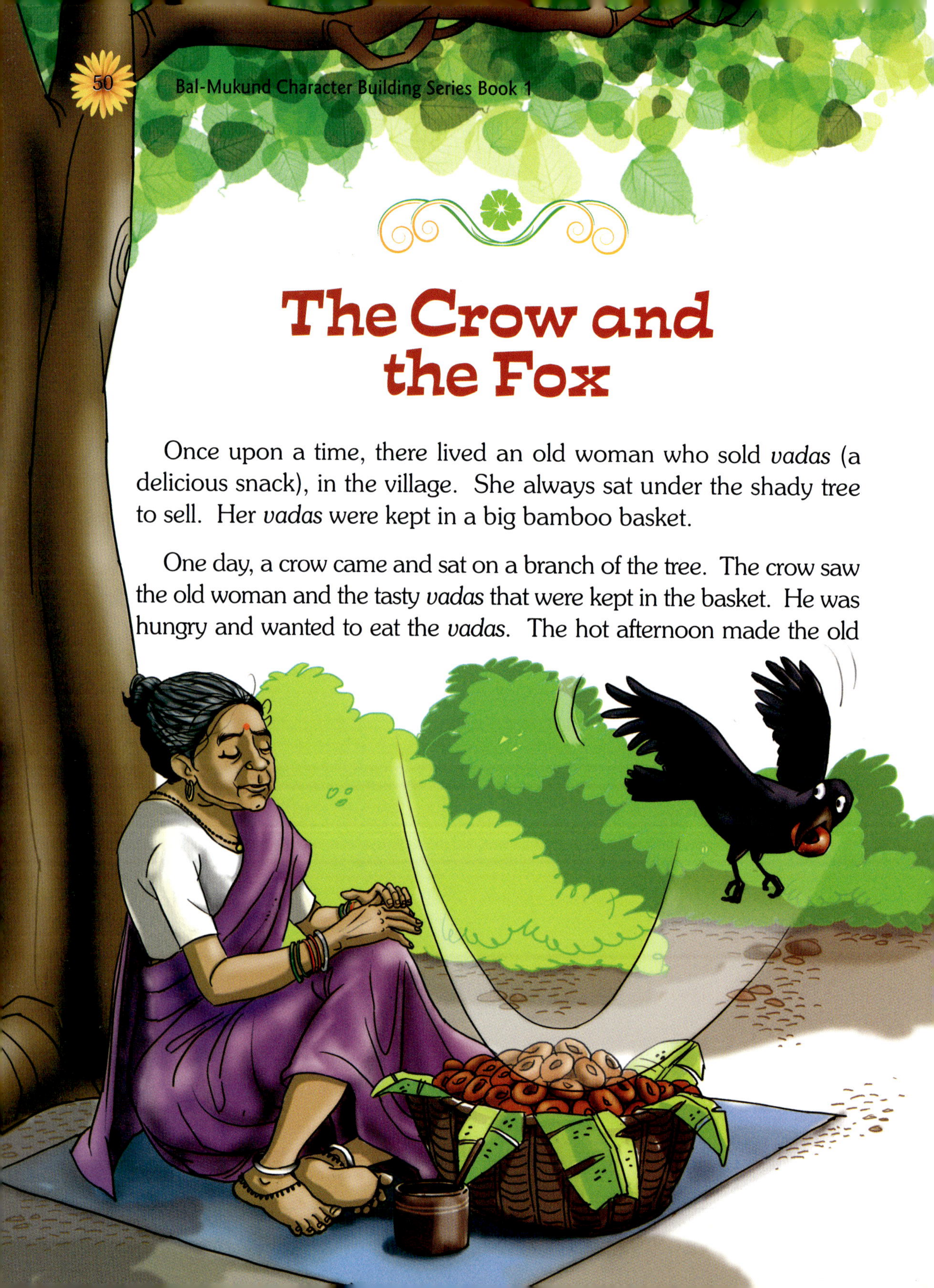

The Crow and the Fox

Once upon a time, there lived an old woman who sold *vadas* (a delicious snack), in the village. She always sat under the shady tree to sell. Her *vadas* were kept in a big bamboo basket.

One day, a crow came and sat on a branch of the tree. The crow saw the old woman and the tasty *vadas* that were kept in the basket. He was hungry and wanted to eat the *vadas*. The hot afternoon made the old

woman sleepy. She decided to take a short nap and the crow noticed this. He flew down from the tree and hopped close to the old woman and her basket. The crow picked a *vada* with his beak and flew away before the old woman could wake up.

With the *vada* in his beak, the crow flew and sat on another branch of the tree. A fox came searching for food and saw the crow and the *vada*. He wanted to eat the *vada* and came up with a wicked plan to steal it.

The fox came and sat under the crow. "Dear crow, I am your greatest admirer. Your voice is so melodious. I have heard you sing many times. Can you sing a song for me?"

The crow believed the fox was truly praising his voice and decided to sing a song. First he cleared his throat and began to sing. As soon as the crow opened his beak the *vada* came falling down to the ground. At once the fox picked the *vada* and ran away into the jungle. Realizing that he had been cheated by the fox, he learned that one should never believe too much praise.

Moral of the story

Do not cheat or mislead others for your own benefit.

The Clever Rabbit and the Angry Lion

Once upon a time, an evil lion ruled the animals in a jungle. All animals feared him and none could match his strength. He hunted and killed for fun, even if he was not hungry. Soon few animals remained in the jungle.

One day, all the animals gathered around the lion's den and begged him to stop his cruelty. "Your majesty," the animals pleaded, "If you kill us while hunting, there will be none left in the jungle to feed you. We suggest you remain in your den while one of us comes to you every day as your meal." The lion thought about what the animals had said. He replied, "I agree to your offer, but if you fail to send me food even for a day, I will kill all of you." The animals agreed.

From that day onwards, one animal sadly made his way to lion's den to be eaten. This continued until it was the rabbit's turn. The rabbit, unlike other animals, was a clever creature. He did not want to be the lion's dinner. He thought for a long time and came up with an idea to save himself and the other animals.

The rabbit set out for the lion's den. He was in no hurry. He took his own time and reached the den late in the evening. The lion meanwhile was very hungry as he had not had anything to eat since morning. Hunger made him angry too. When he saw a small rabbit coming towards him, he roared, "Who sent you here? You are too small to satisfy my hunger and you are late. I shall teach all the animals a lesson for sending you here late. I will kill you all."

The rabbit bowed in respect and said, "Oh King of the jungle! Do not blame me or other animals for what happened. They knew that one rabbit would hardly satisfy your majesty's hunger and sent six rabbits. On our way here, five rabbits were killed and eaten up by another lion. Only I am alive."

"Another lion in my jungle? Who is he? Where did you see him?" questioned the angry lion.

"He is a massive lion, your majesty," said the rabbit. "Jumping out of his cave, he killed five rabbits with his huge claws. He was about to kill me, but I forewarned him, "You have made a big mistake. We were to be the king's dinner and you have spoiled it. Your foolishness will cost your life. Our king will soon kill you."

"Hearing this, he asked me, 'Who is this lion, you talk about? I am the only king of this jungle and the animals are my subjects. Your king must be an impostor. Bring him to me and I shall show him who the real king is.' He let me live to take you to him," explained the rabbit.

On hearing this, the lion roared with such fury that the jungle shook. "Lead me to the place where this fool lives," he said. "I will not rest in peace until I kill the one who has insulted me and eaten my food."

"Your majesty, please come with me," said the rabbit, leading the lion to an abandoned well. "There my Lord!" called out the rabbit pointing at the well, "That is where his fortress lies."

"Where is he?" asked the lion, looking around. "He was right here; this is where I saw him," said the rabbit. "I think, the moment he saw you he must have jumped into his fortress in fear. Come sir, I shall show you." The rabbit asked the lion to look into the well. The lion peeped in and saw his reflection in the well's water.

He was enraged. From inside the well came a louder roar. It was the lion's own voice echoing from the well, but the lion was too infuriated to think clearly. Thinking it was the roar of the other lion he did not wait a second longer. Jumping into the well, he crashed his head against the rocks, fell into the water and drowned.

The clever little rabbit returned home happily and told the other animals how he had gotten rid of the evil lion. The animals of the jungle lived happily ever after, without any fear.

Moral of the story

Moral 1: Intelligence is more powerful than physical strength. Use your intelligence to face difficult situations.

Moral 2: Anger clouds your judgement and prevents the mind from thinking clearly.

The Evil Minded Servant

Birbal, the wisest man in Emperor Akbar's court, helped the king in everything he did.

One day, Birbal went for a walk to the market. He met a rich merchant who said, "Please Sir, I need

your help. I have heard that you are a wise person and can solve any problem. Someone is stealing in my household and I think it is one of my servants. I do not know how to find the thief."

Birbal went to the merchant's house. He called all the servants who worked there. He gave a stick to each of them and said, "I am giving all of you one of these magic sticks. The stick will grow one inch a day in the hands of the person who has been stealing in this house. Come to me tomorrow with this stick and we will find the thief." Birbal was sure that he would find the real thief.

The servant who had been stealing thought, "I must cut an inch from the stick given to me. Tomorrow when it grows, it will be of the same size as the others." He cut the stick by an inch and waited for the next day.

Birbal called all the servants to him the next morning. He checked all the sticks, one by one. The stick of the thief was shorter by an inch when compared with the other sticks. He told the servant, "You are the thief and have been stealing from your master. There was no magic in these sticks. When you cut the stick, you proved you were guilty."

In this way, the merchant was able to identify the thief with the help of wise Birbal. People who steal are finally caught. The servant committed an evil act. This was making him think evil. The guilt made him cut the stick and he gave himself away.

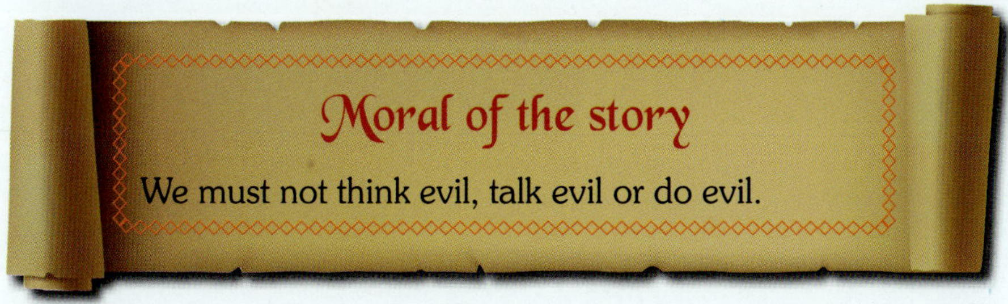

Moral of the story

We must not think evil, talk evil or do evil.

The Unworthy Friends

A group of crows close lived close to a small village. They were friendly to each other and to the birds outside their group. The pack had a few hard working crows and some were idle most of the time. When the idle crows were hungry, they would fly to the neighboring field and steal corns and grains. They satisfied their hunger easily by stealing.

The farmers were fed up with the group of crows. They had become a huge nuisance to the whole village. The farmers were keen to protect the crops they had grown with hard work. They decided to teach crows a lesson and were waiting for the right time.

A man in the village owned a pigeon. She was not given enough food by her master. One day, she was very hungry. She found out that the crows had good food to eat every day. She thought she will ask them where to find food.

She went to the leader of the crows and said, "Dear leader of the crows, you eat good food everyday but I am mostly hungry. Can I join your group? I too would fly with you and enjoy good food everyday."

The leader of the crows talked with others. They agreed that the pigeon should join their group. "I would love to have you in my group. Come with us when we go in search of food," said the leader.

From that day on, the pigeon started flying with the crows. She was never hungry again. Time passed smoothly. She had forgotten her master by then.

One day, as usual, the crows planned to steal grains from a nearby farm. All of them flew to the farm. The pigeon went with them. They swooped greedily on the grains, planning to eat them. The clever farmer had spread a net over the crops. All the crows got caught in the net. The pigeon also got trapped.

The farmer had decided and planned to teach this group a lesson for stealing their crops. The pigeon suffered due to the unworthy group which she was a part of. Though she enjoyed initially and had a good time, it did not last as evil ways generally don't last.

Stealing is a bad habit due to which the entire group suffered. The pigeon thought, "Bad association is bound to land one in trouble some day. Before I joined them, I was fed less and I starved, but I was out of trouble". The pigeon regretted joining the group of crows and decided to give up bad company.

Moral of the story

Doing bad or evil deeds leads us to trouble. Do not associate with bad friends.

The Donkey in a Tiger's Skin

In a small village, there lived a dhobi . His name was Gangaram. He had a wife and seven children. He owned a donkey. The dhobi used the donkey to carry bundles of clothes to and from the river. The donkey worked very hard. The miserly Gangaram did not give the donkey much to eat. The donkey would remain hungry and become weak and thin.

The dhobi thought, "I have so many people in my family. I do not earn much. How can I spend money to feed this animal? I have to find free food or it will become too weak and may die. Then what will I do?"

Once, he was going to another village to meet a friend. On the way, he passed a thick forest that has many wild animals. While resting under a tree, he found a tiger's skin lying on the ground. He picked it up and returned home. Gangaram forgot about the tiger's skin for a while and continued to work hard daily. One fine day, he suddenly came up with an idea to help feed his weak donkey.

That night, he put the tiger's skin on the donkey and took him to the fields near by. He left the donkey there to feed itself. Some farmers were keeping watch on the crops. They saw this animal in their fields, and thinking that it was a tiger, ran away. The donkey ate well that night and returned home early in the morning.

Gangaram had found a cunning way to find free food for his donkey. This act continued for many days. Each night Ganagaram put on the tigers skin on the donkey and left it in the fields. It ate its fill and returned in the morning. The donkey had now become healthy and fat.

One night, while the donkey was feeding on the crops, he heard another donkey braying. Thinking that the other donkey is a friend, he started to bray in a loud voice. The farmers came out of their huts and saw that it was an actually a donkey in a tiger's skin! They were very angry when they realized that the donkey was eating their crops every night. They came out with big sticks and beat the donkey to death.

Alas! The donkey paid a price for his master's lies. Both the donkey and his master had been dishonest. We must remember that lies eventually catch up with us. Honesty and integrity always pays.

Moral of the story

You cannot fool people for long.

P for Perseverance

The Kripalu Value beginning with the letter "P" is Perseverance. The various aspects of perseverance are:

- ❖ Hardworking
- ❖ Enduring
- ❖ Patient
- ❖ Dedication to the work at hand
- ❖ Tenacity to bear difficulties and not give up
- ❖ Overcoming obstacles through persistence
- ❖ Keeping a positive "I can do it" attitude
- ❖ Single-mindedness towards goal
- ❖ Using tact, intelligence and mental power to solve a problem

The Crow and the Pitcher

This is a story of an old wise crow. All the crows in his town looked up to him for advise in times of difficulty. He earned his place as their leader due to his problem solving ability.

Once, an old crow was very thirsty. He had been looking for water all morning. He looked everywhere but could not find water to quench his thirst. Since it had not rained for many weeks, all the small streams and ponds had dried up. At last, he found a pitcher in the garden of a house. He flew to it and saw that there was little water at the bottom of the pitcher. He put his beak into the mouth of the pitcher but could not reach the water. He stretched his neck but still could not drink. He walked to the other side of the pitcher and tried again. It was no use. He was feeling faint and felt he would die of thirst. He thought, "I will break the pitcher and get the water." He thumped the pitcher from all sides. The strong pitcher did not break. He was disappointed but he did not give up.

He took some time to think of another plan. After a while, he thought, "I am big and strong. I will tip the pitcher and get the water." He tried to push the pitcher with his body but it did not move. This made him very sad. All his plans were failing, but he had to find a way to reach the water and quench his thirst.

He did not give up, looked here and there, and saw some pebbles lying near by. Suddenly, he had an idea.

He picked one pebble in his beak and dropped it into the pitcher. Then he dropped some more. He saw the water rising up. He could not believe his eyes. The clever crow kept on dropping pebbles into the pitcher until the water was near the top.

He put his beak into the mouth of the pitcher and was able to reach the water. He quenched his thirst. He felt refreshed and flew away happily.

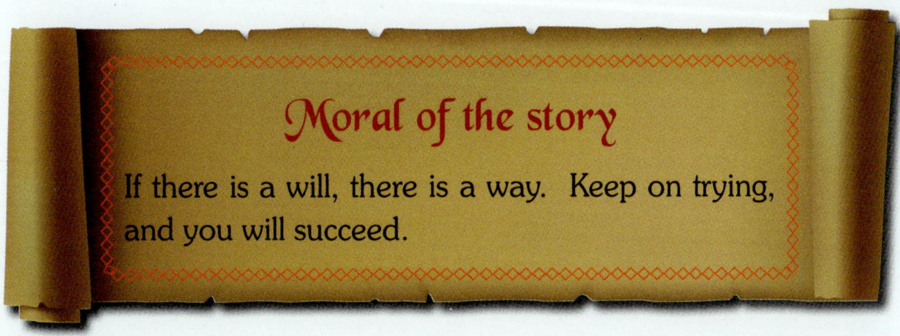

Moral of the story

If there is a will, there is a way. Keep on trying, and you will succeed.

The Rabbit and the Tortoise

Once upon a time, there lived a proud rabbit who hopped around the jungle. None could match his speed. To prove this, he challenged other animals for a race, but the Rabbit always won.

One day, the rabbit saw a tortoise passing by. He was walking slowly. The rabbit had never run a race with a tortoise. He asked him, "Would you like to race me?" The tortoise looked up slowly and nodded his head. "Who will judge the winner?" he asked. They saw the wise old fox and called him.

"We are running a race. Will you be the judge?" the rabbit asked. The

fox agreed. He soon marked the start and finish line for the race. He then asked the rabbit and tortoise to get ready at the starting line. "On your mark, get set and go!" the fox shouted, and the race between the tortoise and the rabbit began.

The rabbit ran fast with his strong legs. The tortoise was left far behind. After the rabbit completed half the race, he turned and looked back. The tortoise was far away from him. "The tortoise is so slow. Even if I sleep a little, I will win the race," thought the proud rabbit. He fell asleep under a shady tree.

The tortoise slowly and steadily continued the race. He did not take any rest. After a long time, he crossed the sleeping rabbit. The tortoise did not disturb him and continued with the race.

By the time the rabbit woke up it was too late. The tortoise was close to the finish line. The rabbit tried to catch up with the tortoise, but he could not. The tortoise finished the race before the rabbit.

The fox declared the tortoise as the winner. The rabbit learned a good lesson from the tortoise.

Moral of the story

Slow and steady wins the race. Do not give up until you reach your goal.

The Doves and the Hunter

A farmer had a paddy field full of grains. A dole of doves was very hungry. While flying in search of food, they saw the field. They were happy to find so much of food all in one place. All of them swooped down on the field and ate up all the grains.

The farmer saw them destroying his grains and he was very angry. He knew he would have to do something, or his field would not be safe. He asked a hunter to help him. He said, "Some doves are destroying the grains in my paddy field. I want you to find a way to catch all of them together." The hunter replied, "Do not worry. I will catch all of them at the same time." The farmer waited to see what was going to happen.

The hunter came with a big net and placed it near the paddy field. The net was filled with grains. The flock of doves saw the grains and flew down to eat them. While eating the grains, they were caught in the net. They tried to free themselves but did not succeed. They were afraid.

Just then, they saw their friend, the crow. He was sitting on a tree branch. "What has happened to you all?" he asked. "We are caught in this hunter's net. We are not able to free ourselves," the doves replied.

The crow thought and said, "If you all act with unity, you can save yourselves. All of you fly together with each one holding on to a little piece of the net. I will lead you to a place which is far from here." The doves did as they were told. The crow called another of his friends to come and help. This was a mouse. The doves flew to the ground with the net. The crow asked the mouse to nibble on the thread of the net. The mouse came and started work. One by one, he cut the net with his teeth and freed all the doves. The doves thanked the crow and the mouse and flew away happily. The loyal friends of the doves solved their problem.

Moral of the story

If you act with unity, you will always be victorious, because unity is strength.

The Monkey and the Crocodile

Uchhal, the monkey lived happily in Pedpur. He had a great time every day jumping from one branch to another. Uchhal would jump from the first tree to the last. Many of these trees were *jamun* (blackberry) trees. They bore fresh, juicy *jamuns,* which Ucchal ate.

The trees were surrounded by a river. Once, when Ucchal was taking his afternoon nap, Chhal the crocodile came out of the river and settled under the tree. Chhal approached Uchhal and asked him to be his friend because he was lonely.

Uchhal was a friendly monkey. He told Chhal, "Since you are my guest today, I should offer you something." Uchhal threw some *jamuns* towards Chhal after finding the best ones.

Chhal liked the *jamuns* and asked for more. Uchhal gave him more. They became friends. Every day in the afternoon, Chhal would come on the shore and Uchhal would give Chhal the *jamuns* he loved so much. They would talk about Pedpur, the pleasant climate, the greenery and the river.

As the days passed, Chhal started taking *jamuns* for his wife at home. Lalchi, his wife loved the jamuns more than Chhal did and told him one day, "If the jamuns are so good, I wonder how sweet the monkey eating those jamuns will taste. Please get the heart of Uchhal for me," she said.

Chhal said it would be unfair to do this to a dear friend. Lalchi got upset and talked Chhal into it. Finally, he thought of a plan.

The next day, when Chhal met Uchhal, he told him, “You know, my wife fought with me.” Curious Uchhal asked, “Why?” Chhal said, “She said that we have been friends for a long time but I have not invited you to our home. Tonight you must have dinner with us.”

Uchhal felt wonderful but since he did not know how to swim, how could he go to Chhal’s home. Chhal solved the problem by saying Uchhal could hop on his back. Uchhal agreed and both of them started moving towards the other end of the river. In the middle of the river, Chhal told the truth to Uchhal. Since Uchhal did not know how to swim, he could not escape.

Chhal told Uchhal, "You know, I am taking you to my wife as she wants your heart. She feels it will be delicious. Since the *jamuns* you eat taste so good, your heart should taste even better."

Uchhal was shocked and felt sad. He knew he was in danger and wondered what to do. After two minutes, he thought of an idea. He told Chhal, "You know friend, it would be a pleasure to offer my heart to your wife. However, and I keep it safely in the burrows of one of the *jamun* trees."

Chhal said, "What do we do then?" Uchhal smartly said, "Just take me to the bank of the river and wait for a few minutes while I get my heart for your loving wife."

Chhal agreed and turned back to the side of the river, unaware of

Uchhal's plan. On the way, Uchhal realized there was no point in being friends with Chhal.

As the two reached the bank of the river, Uchhal quickly jumped from the crocodile's back and climbed up to one of the *jamun* trees. Chhal waited a while but when Uchhal did not come down, he asked, "What is the matter? Pick your heart and come fast. We have to go. My wife must be waiting."

Safely settled on the branch of a big tree, Uchhal told Chhal, "You cheated your friend and now I have cheated you. How could you believe that anyone would keep his heart in the burrows of a tree? It was my escape plan to save myself and also teach a deceiving friend like you a lesson."

He added, "I offered you sweet *jamuns*, but you wanted more." Chhal felt bad and wondered what he would tell his wife Lalchi. He also felt bad for losing a good friend like Uchhal.

Uchhal felt happy because he used his brains at the right time to get out of danger. He thought, "If I use my brain I can stay out of trouble."

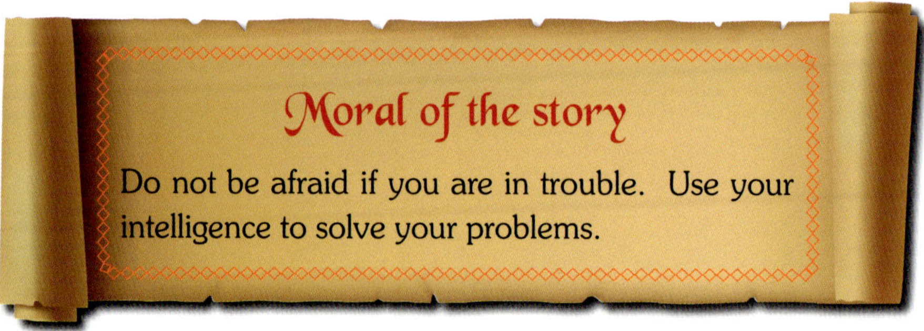

Moral of the story

Do not be afraid if you are in trouble. Use your intelligence to solve your problems.

The Dreamy Milkmaid

Once, there lived a milkmaid. She had some cows that grazed in the meadow.

One day, as usual, she went to the meadow and milked her cows. She kept the pail of milk, on her head. As she started home, she made plans. In her daydream, she thought, "I will make cream and butter out of this milk and sell the butter and cream in the market. With the money I get, I will buy eggs." She further thought, "One day, the eggs will hatch. I will start a nice chicken farm of my own. I will sell some and get enough money to buy a beautiful dress."

Finally she thought, "I will wear my new dress to the fair. All the boys will like me and come after me."

She was so lost in her daydreams that she forgot the pail of milk, which she was carrying on her head. Thinking of the boys coming after her, she thought, "I will not talk to any of them. Just by tossing my head, I will turn them away."

Lost in her plans, she practiced tossing her head. The pail on her head fell down and broke. All the milk tumbled to the ground. "Oh dear!" she cried. "My pail of milk and my dreams are gone."

The milkmaid should have kept her mind on her present work before daydreaming. She should have worked towards her goal slowly and steadily.

Moral of the story

Do not just daydream, work toward your goal.

A for Accountability

The Kripalu value beginning with the letter "A" is Accountability. The various aspects of integrity are:

- ❖ Taking full responsibility for ones deeds
- ❖ Taking the onus for mistakes and the responsibility for correcting them
- ❖ not blaming others or having a whining nature,
- ❖ Taking responsibility for organizing oneself and one's work
- ❖ Accepting the law of karma that what happens to us is a result of our own actions
- ❖ Being punctual to our time commitments

The Dog and a piece of Bone

One day, a dog was walking near the butcher's shop and saw a bone on the ground with some meat on it. The butcher had just thrown it outside his shop. The dog picked up the bone and went to a hidden corner to enjoy the bone. On his way, he growled and

scowled at anyone who tried to take the bone. He did not want to lose the bone and he chewed on it for a long time.

Afterwards he thought, “Let me bury this bone in a safe place in the woods so that I can chew it again.” He came to a river and started crossing the bridge to go to the other side. When he was halfway he thought, “I am so thirsty. Let me drink some water and I will go to bury this bone.”

He thought of keeping the bone on the ground in order to stoop and drink water. When he glanced over the bridge, he found another dog in the water. The dog did not realize that he was seeing his own reflection in the water.

He growled and scowled at it. His own reflection in the water growled and scowled back at him. He thought, “Why don’t I snatch this bone from the other dog’s mouth. That way, I will have two bones to chew. I won’t have to search for food for two days once I get the other bone.”

The dog jumped into the river, barking loudly to get the other dog’s bone. As soon as he started barking, the bone in his mouth fell into the water and disappeared into the river. He lost his bone, and got wet and angry. There was no way he could get the bone back. He realized that there was no other dog there. He had been seeing his own reflection in the water all along. He scolded himself for being a fool.

The dog had become greedy and lost his bone. There was no one to blame but himself. If he had been satisfied with what he had and not been greedy, he would still have his bone.

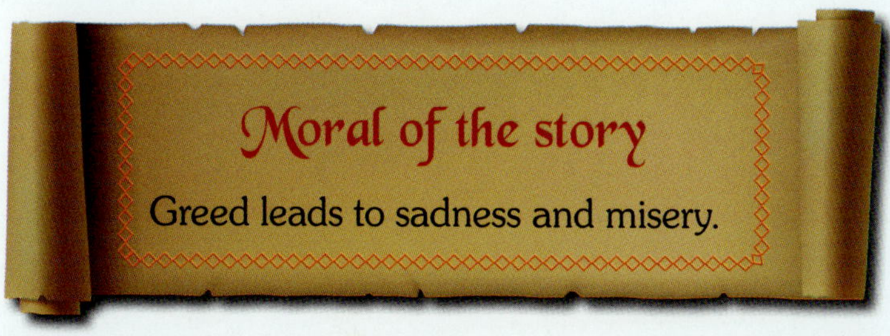

The Shepherd Boy and the Tiger

A shepherd boy lived in a village close to the forest. The shepherd boy was naughty. He liked to play jokes on the villagers, just to bother them. He used to take his sheep for grazing, and would play his flute and sing while his sheep grazed.

It was winter and he had heard the villagers talking about tigers attacking and killing people and animals. One day, he heard that a tiger had carried away a two year old child. He planned to fool the villagers. Next day, when he took his sheep to graze, he suddenly shouted, "Help me! Help me! The tiger is attacking the sheep."

The villagers left their work in the fields and ran to help the boy with sticks in their hands. They noticed that there was no sign of a tiger. The sheep were grazing peacefully. They were very angry. They scolded the boy and went away.

Next day, the shepherd boy shouted again, "Please come and help me! The tiger is here." Some villagers came running to help with sticks in their hands. They asked, "Where is the tiger?" The boy laughingly said, "There is no tiger. I have made a fool of you." The villagers replied, "You are a very naughty boy. You made us come for no reason.

No one will help you." The boy stood shaking with laughter.

After a few days, while the boy was near the forest with his sheep, a tiger attacked them. The scared boy stood on a wall and screamed with fear, "Help! Help! The tiger is eating my sheep. Please hurry and come."

The villagers heard the boy, but did not come. "It must be the silly boy trying to make a fool of us again. We will not fall for his joke this time."

The tiger was too fierce and strong for the boy. It killed and ate the sheep, and then attacked the boy too. In the end, the shepherd boy lost his life too because of his habit of making a fool of others.

This goes to show that lying to people is a bad habit because lies will catch up with you in the end. Liars get punished by their own words and actions, because people come to know and stop believing them. If you try to make a fool of others, you will yourself get into trouble. That is why we should develop the habit of speaking the truth in our lives and earn the respect of others.

Although, the shepherd boy was telling the truth the third time, no one believed him because he had lied twice before. He had to face the consequences of his own actions. We are accountable for our words and actions. If we are honest, we need not worry. If we do bad things to others, we will get punished.

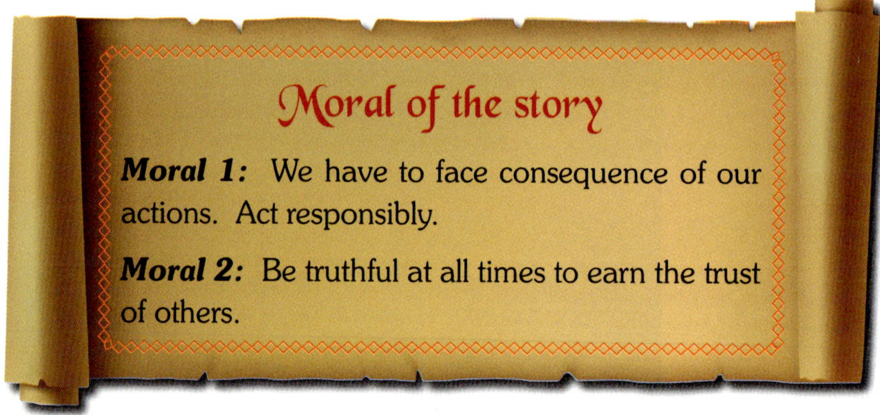

Moral of the story

Moral 1: We have to face consequence of our actions. Act responsibly.

Moral 2: Be truthful at all times to earn the trust of others.

The Donkey's Load

There lived a merchant near the seashore who owned a donkey. One day, he decided to buy salt from the market. He went and bought large bags of salt and loaded them on

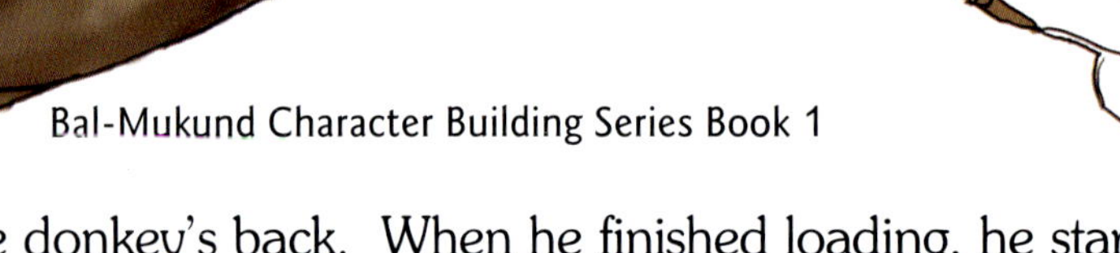

the donkey's back. When he finished loading, he started home. On the way, they had to cross a river. The merchant had crossed this river with his donkey many times before. When they reached the middle of the river, the animal took a false step, stumbled and fell into the river. The salt dissolved into the river's water. When he got up to go, he found that his load was much lighter.

The donkey thought to himself, "This is a good way to make my load lighter. I can fall on purpose each time my master makes me carry heavy things". He walked along happily after that.

Next day, the merchant went to get salt. While coming back, halfway on the river, the donkey purposely fell down. Again the salt dissolved in the water and the donkey went home with a much lighter load. This time, his master saw through his trick. He felt bad about all the salt that was wasted due to the donkey's tricks and wanted to make sure that the donkey would not do this again. He thought that simply scolding the donkey would not help. He had to find a way to teach him a lesson that he would not forget.

After a few days, the merchant visited the market again. This time he bought cotton. He loaded cotton bales on the donkey's back. While crossing the river, the donkey tried his old trick and fell down on purpose. This time the cotton bales became soaked with a lot of water and became twice as heavy. The poor animal had trouble getting up after his fall. He felt like dying with his heavy load and felt sorry for himself.

We see that the donkey tried to trick his master by being too smart. He had to pay for his tricks and carry a much heavier load the next time.

We should always think before we act. Whatever happens to us in life is the result of our own doings. If we do good deeds, we are rewarded. However, we have to pay for our mistakes and wrong doings. We have to take responsibility for what we do in life. If we try to trick and fool others, we will be caught.

The donkey tried to be clever. He thought that he could make his load lighter, each time he crossed the river by falling down on purpose. The lesson he learned was "Don't make your work easier at the cost of loss to others."

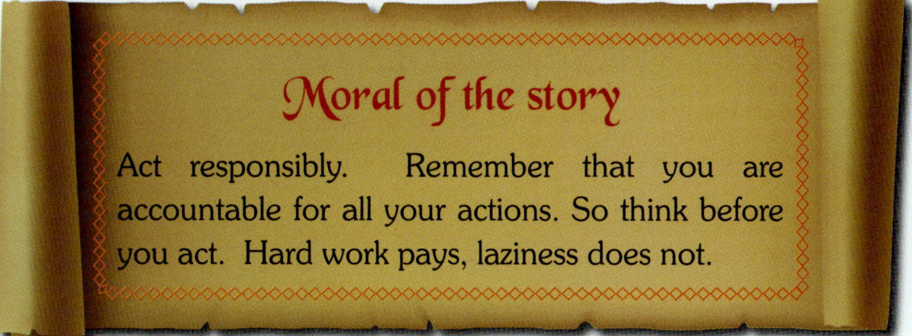

The Fox and the Grapes

Chutki, the fox was very hungry. She searched for food in the jungle but could not find anything to eat. It was almost afternoon and she had eaten nothing. While she was looking here and there for something she could eat, she came across a grapevine. Bunches of nice and juicy grapes hung from the grapevine. The juicy grapes made Chutki's mouth water. The

grapevine was not easily reachable and Chutki would have to jump hard to catch the grapes.

Since Chutki was hungry and badly wanted the grapes to satisfy her hunger, she was ready to jump and reach them. The first time Chutki jumped, she missed the grapes by a tall margin. She realized she would have to jump higher and put in more effort.

She tried for the second time but again missed the target and could not even touch the lower end of the bunch. Chutki felt tired but tried for the third time with more energy. This time, she managed to touch the grapes but could not pluck the bunch.

Chutki tried again but, every time she tried, she just managed to feel the grapes without being able to grab them.

Chutki did not want to accept that she was unable to get them. At the same time she had given up and did not want to try harder. So Chutki found an excuse for her failure and put the blame on something else. "The grapes must be sour," she said.

Moral of the story

Keep trying and do not give up easily. Do not make excuses for your failure.

The Ant and the Grasshopper

Murkha was a lazy grasshopper who never liked to work. He always spent his time enjoying the present, never worrying about the future. He would buzz around and hum the songs he liked. Cheeti, the small ant, was the opposite. She always worked hard so she could store enough for winter.

It was the end of the day and Cheeti was still gathering food for the winter. When Murkha saw Cheeti working so much, he said, "Why do you work so hard? The sun is out for us. Let us enjoy my tunes in the bright sunshine. This is what life is all about."

Cheeti continued with her work and replied, "Sunny days will not stay forever. I am gathering the food I will need for the winter season, which is not very far away. I am also building a warm house which will provide me shelter during the cold."

Murkha said, "Come on. The winter is a long time away." He continued to play and made fun of Cheeti who continued to work hard. The days passed by. Murkha the grasshopper did not work at all while Cheeti worked day in and day out.

Soon it was winter and Murkha the grasshopper began getting cold. Cheeti was resting in her warm house, not affected by the snow and the cold. Murkha, the grasshopper, was knocking at her door. “Cheeti, please help me. I need some corn. I have nothing to eat.”

Cheeti replied, “You sang all summer and never bothered to work. Now dance your way through the winter.” Poor Murkha stood helpless. There was severe fog and he could not hum anything but sad songs. He could not think of dancing because his cold feet trembled and shivered. Murkha paid a price for being silly when he could have worked hard and been prepared for the winter season.

Moral of the story

Do not be lazy. If you work hard, you will be prepared.

The Crooked Thinkers

Mandu, Sandhu and Bandhu were thieves who robbed in different parts of Siddhi town. Each of them had a certain gift. Mandu was good at opening locks, Sandhu was good at making fake documents and Bandhu used his knife to escape immediately after committing a robbery.

Once, the three robbers looted a house in Siddhi and escaped with a big sack of precious diamonds, jewels and some cash. Since there was heavy security and many guards kept a close watch, they had no time to sell the jewels and other precious stones.

They quickly escaped into a nearby forest and deposited the sack below a jasmine plant so they could identify it when they wanted to use it. After things quietened down a little and they were sure that nobody was chasing them anymore, the three robbers thought about going back to the town.

They became hungry and decided that one among them would get the food for the other two. Sandhu was given this job. While Sandhu was away getting the food, Mandu and Bandhu thought of keeping the treasure to themselves. Mandu said, "If we beat Sandhu with heavy sticks when he comes back, we can avoid sharing the treasure with him."

The same thought came to Sandhu's mind when he was getting the food. He thought, "Why not keep the whole treasure for myself? If I mix poison in the food, I won't have to share the treasure."

It was clear that to the thieves the money meant more than friendship. Each of them thought of a plan to cheat and even kill the others. Sandhu put poison in the food meant to be eaten by Mandu and Bandhu. When he was almost close to the meeting place, Mandu and Bandhu could see his shadow. They got ready with the sticks and immediately beat Sandhu as planned. Sandhu died instantly.

Mandu and Bandhu were not aware that their end was near. A few minutes after they began eating the food, the poison started to act. Within a short while, Mandu and Bandhu were dead.

None of the three selfish robbers lived to enjoy the stolen jewels and money.

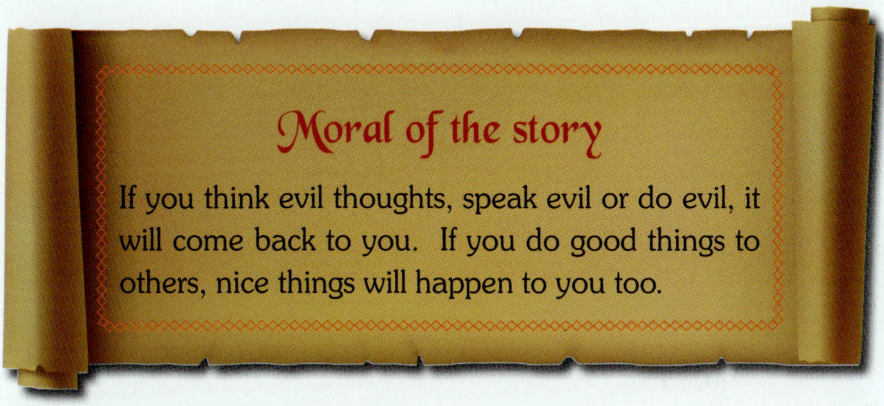

L for Love for God

The Kripalu Value beginning with the letter "L" is love for God. The various aspects of Love for God are:

- ❖ Trust in God
- ❖ Faith in His protection
- ❖ Acceptance of His will
- ❖ Keeping a positive attitude in every situation with faith in God's Grace
- ❖ A sense of gratitude for all that God has given us
- ❖ Belief that He is with us and watching us always
- ❖ Doing all actions for His pleasure
- ❖ Unconditional devotion to Him

Gajendra

Indradyumna was a king known for his virtues. His ways were honest and he was concerned for his subjects. He was deeply spiritual. Once, he called a meeting of his ministers and told them that he wanted to live in the forest to devote all his time in worshipping Lord.

The King went to the Kulachal Mountains and made his home in a small cottage. He observed a vow of silence and immersed himself in meditation of Lord Vishnu. One day, Sage Agastya came to the Kulachal Mountains with his disciples. On seeing Indradyumna not reacting or welcoming them, sage Agastya mistook it for pride. He cursed Indradyumna in anger and turned him into an elephant. Lord Vishnu witnessed this from *Vaikunth* (His Divine abode), and smiled.

Having become an elephant, King Indradyumna began roaming in the forest. Once he came across a big herd of elephants. To be accepted by the other elephants of the gang, Indradyumna defeated the head elephant. He was crowned the new leader of the herd, and came to be known as Gajendra. One day, Gajendra decided to move with his herd to Trikuta Mountains, which he considered a better place than Kulachal.

After storming their way through the Trikuta forest, the herd of elephants proceeded towards a lake. They were not aware that it was a crocodile's home. The crocodile did not like the herd entering his place. In a mood to attack, he moved towards Gajendra. Deciding to teach Gajendra a lesson, the crocodile caught hold of Gajendra's leg. The faithful herd of elephants tried to save their leader but no matter how hard they tried, were no match to the immense strength the crocodile seemed to posses. Eventually they gave up and Gajendra requested they move on without him, as he did not want to put the rest of the herd in danger.

The crocodile was sinking his teeth so hard in Gajendra's leg that the pain became unbearable. He tried his best to free his leg from the crocodile's grasp, but did not succeed. Finally, he turned to Lord Vishnu and humbly surrendered himself in devotion to Him. He called out to the Lord with his sincere prayer to come and rescue him.

On hearing his devotee's prayer, Lord Vishnu immediately left *Vaikunth* and mounting on Garuda, rushed down to earth to rescue

him. Lord Vishnu released his discus and struck the crocodile like lightning, freeing Gajendra's leg. Gajendra was overjoyed to see his Lord, and offering a lotus flower, paid obeisance to Him. Lord Vishnu blessed Gajendra and with His Divine touch, and the elephant King regained his human form as Indradyumna. He thanked Lord Vishnu for protecting him and requested the Lord to take him to *Vaikunth*. This is how Gajendra, the elephant King attained God with his devotion.

Moral of the story

A sincere prayer of the devotee does not go unanswered by the Lord. Always keep God in your thoughts and believe that he will protect you at all times.

King Ambarish

King Ambarish was a just king and a great devotee of Lord Vishnu. Once, he kept a fast, called *Ekadashi Vrat*. He spent the day praying and meditating upon Lord Vishnu. The next day, as the moment of breaking the fast was drawing near, the mighty sage Durvasa arrived.

Ambarish received him with all respect and requested him to be his honored guest at the meal. Durvasa agreed to the king's request, and asked him to wait until he finished his bath in the river and returned. The auspicious moment to break the fast was approaching, and Durvasa had not returned.

Ambarish was in a difficult situation. If he did not eat in time, his fast would be in vain. If he did eat before offering to Durvasa, it would be disrespectful to his guest. Sage Vasishta advised him to merely drink water and a Tulsi leaf. In this way, he would not be eating before his guest, but the fast would be considered broken.

Ambarish followed sage Vasishta's advice and broke his fast by taking a Tulsi leaf and water. However, by his special powers, Durvasa came to know what had happened. When he returned, he was furious. "You have insulted me," shouted Durvasa. "You have had lunch before my arrival. You do not know how to treat a guest."

"Dear Sage, I have not had any food. I only drank water. We shall have our lunch together," said king Ambarish. However, Durvasa was not willing to listen, and said, "I will punish you for this." From a strand of his hair, he created a demon to kill Ambarish.

Seeing the demon come towards him, king Ambarish folded his hands and prayed to Lord Vishnu. Without a moment's delay, the Sudarshan Chakra (Divine disc) of Lord Vishnu appeared. It first killed the demon, and then started chasing Durvasa. The poor sage ran for his life. He tried hiding in caves and crossing rivers but the *chakra* (disc) was right behind him.

At last, Durvasa became very tired and ran to Lord Brahma for help. Brahma replied, "I cannot help you. You have insulted Lord Vishnu's devotee and He is very angry with you." Durvasa then turned to Lord Shiv for help. "It is Lord Vishnu's *chakra*," said Lord Shiv. "Go to him for help. I cannot help you."

So Durvasa turned to Lord Vishnu and said, "Dear Lord, please forgive me. Please protect me from your *chakra*." Lord Vishnu said, "You have insulted my devotee. Only if he forgives you will the *chakra* stop chasing you." Durvasa ran to king Ambarish and begged him for his forgiveness. "O, King I am sorry, I insulted you. Please save me from the *chakra* or it will cut my head."

King Ambarish prayed to Lord Vishnu and the chakra vanished. Thanking the king, Durvasa asked, "I went to Brahma, Shiva and Lord Vishnu for protection. They could not help. How could you? What power do you have?"

King Ambarish replied, "I have the power of Lord Vishnu's love. That is why He protected me, and on my request He got rid of the *chakra* that was chasing you." Hearing this everyone around king Ambarish praised him for his devotion to the Lord.

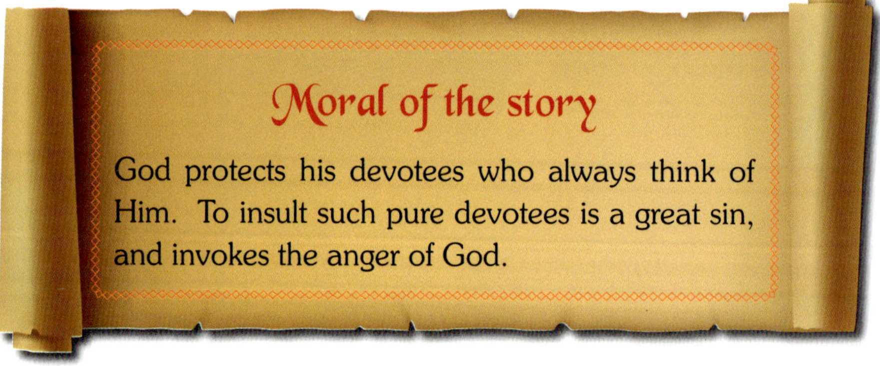

Moral of the story

God protects his devotees who always think of Him. To insult such pure devotees is a great sin, and invokes the anger of God.

Rantidev

Once, the celestial gods in heaven decided to reward most loyal devotee of the Supreme Lord Shree Vishnu. Indra, Brahma, Yamraj and other gods went to Lord Vishnu and asked Him, "Please tell us who your most loyal devotee is?" Lord Vishnu immediately replied, "Rantidev."

Brahma wanted to confirm Lord Vishnu's answer. He asked, "You mean Rantidev, who gave up his royal life of a king and who has been fasting for the past forty-five days, chanting Your name?" "Yes," replied Lord Vishnu.

The celestial gods were not convinced. They wanted to put Rantidev to test. Lord Brahma said, "A hungry man cannot part with his food. Let me test him tomorrow when he will end his fast. As planned, the celestial gods went to Rantidev who was about to break his fast. Placed in front of him was a dish of food and a glass of water. As he was about to put the first morsel into his mouth, a beggar appeared in front of Rantidev and said, "Oh kind man, please give me some food. I have not had food for so many days." Rantidev offered half the food on his plate to the beggar. Lord Vishnu smiled, as he knew Rantidev would pass this test. The beggar thanked Rantidev and continued on his journey.

However, just as Rantidev was about to start eating the rest of the food in the plate, another beggar came and asked Rantidev for food. "Please give me a morsel. I have been starving for many days."

Rantidev gave some of the remaining food in the plate to the second beggar without getting annoyed. When Rantidev started to resume his lunch, a nomad came to him and said, "Please spare some food for my dog and me." Rantidev was left with very little food after satisfying the two beggars. Even then, he did not hesitate in giving away all the food left to the nomad and his dog. The celestial gods, in order to test Rantidev had taken these different forms. They were happy with the results of the test and together said, "We agree; Rantidev is fit to be Lord Vishnu's most loyal devotee. He has passed our tests."

However, Yamraj was not convinced yet. He said, "I want to test him. Only after passing that test will I come to the conclusion." While Rantidev was now left with no food, he was about to break his fast by drinking some water, Yamraj came to him in the form of a poor man. "I am very thirsty. Can I have some water please?" Rantidev immediately fulfilled the request. He offered his water to the thirsty man. Yamraj was amazed by Rantidev's devotion to Lord Vishnu and his act of humanity and kindness.

As soon as the poor man drank the water, all celestial gods came before Rantidev in their true forms. They asked Rantidev how he was able to spare the food and water for beggars and poor people, when he himself was so hungry and thirsty. Rantidev was surprised to see them, but he bowed with humility to all of them. He said, "I see God in all living beings. When I shared my food and water, I was merely serving God."

Lord Vishnu also appeared before Rantidev. Lord Vishnu said, "Rantidev, I am pleased with you. You are certainly fit and deserving to receive my Grace." Rantidev humbly bowed in front of his Lord and sought His blessings.

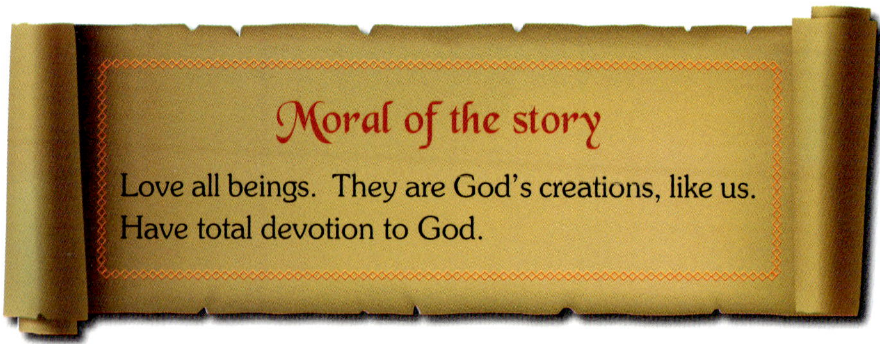

Dhruv

Long ago, there lived a King named Uttanapad. He had two wives, Suniti and Suruchi, and two sons. Suniti's son was Dhruv and Suruchi's son was Uttam. They were both five years old. King Uttanapad was very fond of his younger queen Suruchi, so he stayed with her. He rarely went to Suniti. Dhruv, the elder queen's son, loved his father. So, Dhruv used to visit his father often. Suruchi did not like this. She wanted the king to love only her son. In course of time, the king realized that his younger queen did not like Dhruv.

One day, Dhruv saw his brother Uttam sitting in his father's lap and playing. He rushed to give him a hug and sit on his lap too. Queen Suruchi stopped him and said, "You are not my son, so you shall not sit on your father's lap." On hearing this, Dhruv was very hurt. With tears in his eyes, he went home to his mother.

Queen Suniti was very sad to hear what had happened to her son. Dhruv asked her why his father loved him less. She comforted him and replied unhappily, "The king loves Queen Suruchi and not me. So, the king does what she wants, and neglects you. I am helpless."

"Mother, is there no other way I can get my father's love?" asked Dhruv. His mother Suniti consoled and instructed little Dhruv:

1. If you have to beg for something, let that be from God.
2. However much you ask of a human being, it will be little.
3. Suruchi has spoken words of truth, even if you want the throne, pray to the Lord!
4. When God gives, He gives in plenty.
5. God is the true Father of us all. He will make you sit on His lap with love.
6. If you get a vision of Lord Narayan, all your troubles will end.
7. Go to the forest and perform penance.
8. I am not sending you alone, my blessings and God are with you.

Hearing this, Dhruv decided to seek Lord Narayan. He took his mother's blessings and left for the jungle, dressed in simple clothes. On his way, he met Narad, the closest devotee of Lord Narayan. Sage Narad tested Dhruv, "It is not easy to meet Narayan. You are very young.

Go and play with your friends instead." Dhruv was very determined to see Lord Narayan at any cost. His determination pleased Narad, who taught Dhruv the *sadhana* (spiritual practice) that would help him see the Lord.

After teaching Dhruv, Narad met King Uttanapad in the palace. Narad gave him news about Dhruv. He also told him that Dhruv would soon return to the kingdom after receiving Lord Narayan's blessings. The king was glad to hear that his son was safe. He realized his mistake and promised to treat both his queens and sons equally and affectionately.

Dhruv started worshiping Lord Narayan. For the first month, he lived only on fruits. After that, he lived on leaves and water. Finally, he lived on air alone. The penance was so intense that it heated up all the worlds. Devotees rushed to Lord Narayan and prayed to him to pacify Dhruv by granting him his wish.

Lord Narayan was pleased with Dhruv's penance. He appeared before him and blessed him, "O child! Your father and all the others will love you dearly hereafter. Go back to your kingdom. You will become a great king and rule your kingdom for a long time. After your life on the earth, you will become the Dhruv star and shine brightly in the sky. All the great planets and even the seven great *rishis* will revolve around you."

Even today, Dhruv is remembered as a great devotee of Lord Narayan.

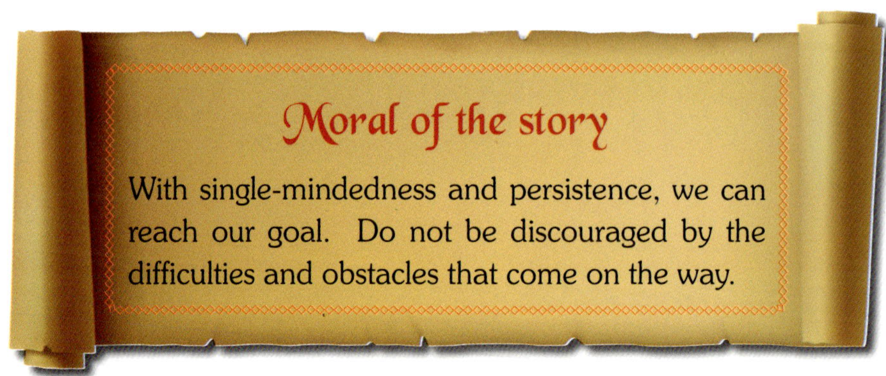

Moral of the story

With single-mindedness and persistence, we can reach our goal. Do not be discouraged by the difficulties and obstacles that come on the way.

U for Unassuming

The Kripalu value beginning with the letter "U" is Unassuming. The various aspects of being unassuming are:

- ❖ Modesty
- ❖ Unpretentiousness
- ❖ Simplicity
- ❖ Humility
- ❖ Not boasting or showing off
- ❖ Reverence for the Greatness of God
- ❖ Faith that everything belongs to God and not to us
- ❖ Realizing that God has a grand scheme why things happen and we all have a tiny role to play in His design

The Oak Tree and the Reeds

The Oak tree was proud of its strength. It often boasted about its strong structure and its firm position. Once it saw the reeds in the river sway from side-to-side by the force of the mighty wind and the flow of the water. The Oak tree said, "Look at me. I stand firm no matter if it rains or strong winds blow. On the other hand, you bow your heads and tilt to the other side whenever the slightest force is used."

The reeds did not like the Oak tree's remarks. However, they did not say anything. They ignored his insulting remarks, and thought, "This is the way we are, and there is nothing wrong in it. Is not every creature different from others? Everyone and everything has its strength and weakness."

Late that night when the Oak tree was laughing loudly and mocking the reeds, a fierce storm arose. The entire village was affected by it. Gushy winds continued to blow for a long time, and several of the Oak tree's branches and leaves fell to the ground. The reeds were noticing the damage caused to the tree by the storm.

The Oak tree was still confident that nothing would happen to it. However, one hour later, the force of the winds increased and the strongest branches of the trees started creaking under the mighty winds. Just a few minutes later, all the Oak tree's branches gave way to the ground and its roots began feeling the force of the storm.

The reeds were surprised to see what had happened to the Oak tree's branches. They asked the Oak tree, "Do you still think you are strong and firm and nothing can topple you?" The Oak tree said, "Yes, of course!"

When the Oak tree's roots started moving, the reeds could hear a loud noise. The strong tree was no longer standing upright, as its trunk was falling on one side. The roots were breaking and getting pulled out of the ground.

The reeds noticed how the strong Oak tree was so weak against the storm. Just then, they heard the tree falling to the ground, broken and uprooted.

When it lay helpless on the earth, the reeds collectively told the Oak tree, "We may bow our heads but we don't break." The humble reeds lasted longer than the proud Oak tree.

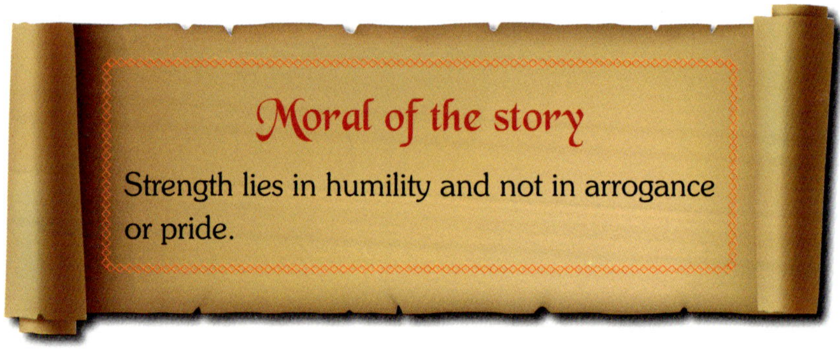

The Sage and the Mouse

Vidyadhar, the wise sage, daily meditated under the *peepal* tree at Sanskarpur. He taught moral values to all animals in the village. Everyone regularly attended his sessions to become better living beings. All the animals gathered around the *peepal* tree and listened to the sage's advice.

Nanha, the mouse, was a regular follower of Vidyadhar and liked the way the sage taught things that changed the animals' lives. Once, when Nanha was returning after attending Vidyadhar's session, he saw a bee fall in a river. Nanha immediately took a leaf and put it in the river. The bee climbed on the leaf and was saved which made Nanha feel good inside.

However, Nanha was not aware that while he was doing this kind act, a big fat cat called Billo was watching him from a distance. She told herself, "What a nice meal I will have today!" The bee overheard this and told Nanha about it.

Worried about his life, the mouse went to the sage. The sage heard Nanha's worries and turned him into a bigger cat than Billo. Nanha felt good on taking the form of a bigger cat and moved around freely. He could now fearlessly go to the river to drink water. The smaller animals whom the mouse feared earlier now stepped back when they saw him.

Life went well for Nanha for a few days. However, one day a fox pounced upon him. Out of fear, Nanha ran for his life. He rushed to Vidyadhar for a solution. Vidyadhar realized that Nanha would not be totally safe even in the form of a cat, and he turned him into a fox.

Being a fox was an experience Nanha enjoyed. Most of the animals were now scared of him. A few days later, a tiger attacked Nanha. Though Nanha escaped and saved himself, he was afraid once again. He went to the wise sage with the problem. The sage thought turning Nanha into a tiger would solve the problem once and for all. He made Nanha from a fox to a tiger. Nanha–the tiger was a happy animal, going around freely in the jungle without fear. Everything went smoothly and Nanha–the tiger was enjoying his life. All the animals were frightened of him. No one dared to bother him in any way.

Alas! Things took an ugly turn. Something happened that the sage had never expected. Nanha-the tiger was roaring loudly. Forgetting

the good that the sage had done to him, Nanha was getting ready to attack him. The sage was shocked by the turn of events. He quickly decided to turn the tiger into a mouse again.

Moral of the story

Be humble and grateful to those who help you.

Bhakt Prahlad

Once Lord Vishnu, in the form of a boar, killed the demon Hiranyaksha and rescued Mother Earth. Hiranyaksha's elder brother Hiranyakashipu, the king of demons, was angry when he heard the news. He desired to take revenge with Lord Vishnu for killing his brother. He went to the Himalayas and did penance to please Lord Brahma. Seeing his severe penance, Brahma asked him what he desired. "O Brahma! Grant me the boon that I should never be killed by any weapon or creature created by you. I should not die in the day or night, on earth or in the sky." Lord Brahma granted him his wish.

After King Hiranyakashipu returned from the Himalayas, his wife Queen Kayadhu gave birth to a son. They named him Prahlad. He was the youngest among Hiranyakashipu's four sons.

Prahlad had many divine qualities. Since childhood, he was always devoted to Lord Vishnu. He did not have any worldly desires and he was always truthful. He wished the best for everyone. He did not have the demonic qualities of his father and brothers. Hiranyakashipu did not like his son worshiping his enemy Lord Vishnu. He tried to stop Prahlad many times, but failed to convince him. He finally decided to kill his son because he did not obey him.

He gave the task to two sages, Shand and Amark. They created a giant monster called Kritya to kill Prahlad, but Kritya destroyed the sages instead of killing Prahlad. Being a kindhearted boy, Prahlad prayed to Lord Vishnu and brought the sages back to life.

King Hiranyakashipu had a sister named Holika. She could not be harmed by fire. Shand and Amark asked her to sit on a bonfire with Prahlad on her lap, hoping that the fire would kill Prahlad. Prahlad was not at all worried. He chanted Lord Vishnu's name and came out of the fire unhurt. Instead, Holika was burnt to death. Everything the demons tried failed in killing Prahlad.

Hiranyakashipu began to feel afraid and sent Prahlad to a school for demon children. However, Prahlad gathered his classmates and preached about God. "Brothers, this human life is meant for finding God. We can even achieve this in our childhood. It is very easy to find God, because He is present in everyone's hearts. Since He is there in every living being, we should never harm other creatures. We should always think that God resides in them."

His teachers saw that Prahlad was behaving against the wishes of his father and sent him back home. Finally, King Hiranyakashipu tied Prahlad to a pillar and said angrily, "Since you have disobeyed me, I am going to kill you. Call your God to save you." Prahlad replied, "Father, do not be angry, and I am not disobeying you. Lord Vishnu is the protector of us all. He is everywhere. He is in me; He is in you; He is in your sword, and He is also present in this pillar."

His angry father laughed and hit the pillar with his war club. As soon as it touched the pillar, it broke with a thundering sound. A creature came out from the pillar. He had the face of a lion and the body of a human. He was Lord Vishnu in the form of Narasingh. He roared angrily.

Lord Narasingh caught Hiranyakashipu and dragged him towards the doorstep. He put Hiranyakashipu on his thighs and tore his belly with his nails. Prahlad then laid himself at the feet of his Lord. Affectionately, Lord Narasingh raised him and said, "You had to bear many sufferings, but you did not give up your devotion. I am very pleased with you." Prahlad bowed his head faithfully.

Lord Narasingh then asked Prahlad to seek a boon. Prahlad said, "You are my Lord, and if you wish to grant me a boon, kindly bless me that I may have no desires." Prahlad also prayed that Lord Narasingh would forgive his father. Lord Narasingh replied, "The power of your devotion has wiped away the sins of your father. He has already been saved."

Lord Narasingh led Prahlad to the throne of his father and crowned him king. He instructed him to follow good conduct and do his duties faithfully. Saying this, Lord Vishnu in Narasingh's form returned to His abode.

Prahlad is the finest example of devotion to God. Even though people with bad thoughts and deeds surrounded him, Prahlad remembered God. Though his father was a demon, Prahlad was not against him. He was kind to everyone, including the people who tried to kill him. His love for God was strong. One can achieve great goals with love and devotion for God.

BAL-MUKUND CHARACTER BUILDING SERIES

1. Inspiring Stories for Children, Vol 1
2. Inspiring Stories for Children, Vol 2
3. Inspiring Stories for Children, Vol 3
4. Inspiring Stories for Children, Vol 4
5. Festivals of India
6. Saints of India
7. The Bal-Mukund WISDOM Book
8. The Bal-Mukund Painting Book

Audio CDs

1. The Bal-Mukund WISDOM Book-Prayers and Keertans
2. The Bal-Mukund WISDOM Book-Shlokas & Verses
3. Bal-Mukund Meditation for Children